Neighborhood Safari

Squirrels

by Martha London

www.focusreaders.com

Focus Readers is distributed by North Star Editions: sales@northstareditions.com | 888-417-0195

Produced for Focus Readers by Red Line Editorial.

Photographs ©: Shutterstock Images, cover, 1, 4, 9, 13, 17, 21 (squirrel); iStockphoto, 7, 10, 18; Phil McLean/FLPA/Science Source, 14; Red Line Editorial, 21 (chart)

Library of Congress Cataloging-in-Publication Data
Names: London, Martha, author.
Title: Squirrels / Martha London.
Description: Lake Elmo, MN : Focus Readers, [2021] | Series: Neighborhood
  safari | Includes index. | Audience: Grades 2-3
Identifiers: LCCN 2020008228 (print) | LCCN 2020008229 (ebook) | ISBN
  9781644933572 (hardcover) | ISBN 9781644934333 (paperback) | ISBN
  9781644935859 (pdf) | ISBN 9781644935095 (ebook)
Subjects: LCSH: Squirrels--Juvenile literature.
Classification: LCC QL737.R68 L627 2021 (print) | LCC QL737.R68 (ebook) |
  DDC 599.36/2--dc23
LC record available at https://lccn.loc.gov/2020008228
LC ebook record available at https://lccn.loc.gov/2020008229

Printed in the United States of America
Mankato, MN
082020

About the Author

Martha London writes books for young readers. When she's not writing, you can find her hiking in the woods.

Table of Contents

Chapter 1

In the Park

A squirrel carries an acorn in its mouth. The squirrel digs a hole. It **buries** the acorn in the dirt.

Squirrels are **mammals**. They live in many places around the world. Squirrels make their homes in trees. But they bury food in the ground. They eat the buried food during winter.

Fun Fact

Squirrels can find food buried under 12 inches (30 cm) of snow.

Planting Forests

A squirrel collects thousands of nuts and acorns each year. But it does not eat all of them. The squirrel forgets about some. In fact, more than half of the nuts stay buried. These nuts grow into trees. In this way, squirrels plant thousands of trees each year.

Chapter 2

Bushy Tails

Squirrels have long, **bushy** tails. These tails help squirrels stay warm. So does their fur. A squirrel's fur can be many colors, including black, gray, or red.

Squirrels have sharp claws. Their claws help them climb. They grip the tree bark.

Squirrels have large front teeth. Squirrels use them to **gnaw**. They also crack hard shells of nuts and seeds.

Chapter 3

Up a Tree

Squirrels make nests in trees. They gather **twigs** and leaves. Squirrels often build nests between branches. They also use holes in trees.

Squirrels sleep in their nests. They come out to look for food. Squirrels mainly eat nuts and berries. A strong sense of smell helps them find food. Squirrels often live in forests, parks, or yards.

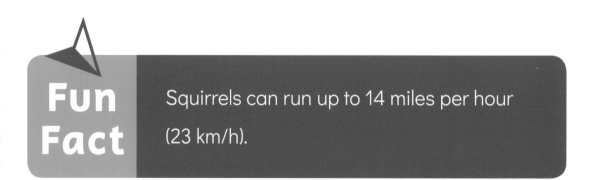

Fun Fact

Squirrels can run up to 14 miles per hour (23 km/h).

Chapter 4

Ready for Winter

To **prepare** for winter, squirrels eat and store lots of food. They build up fat. This fat gives them energy.

Squirrels also grow thicker fur. They stay warm inside their nests. Squirrels use nests to raise their babies, too. Many squirrels give birth in late winter. By spring, the babies are big enough to live on their own.

Life Cycle

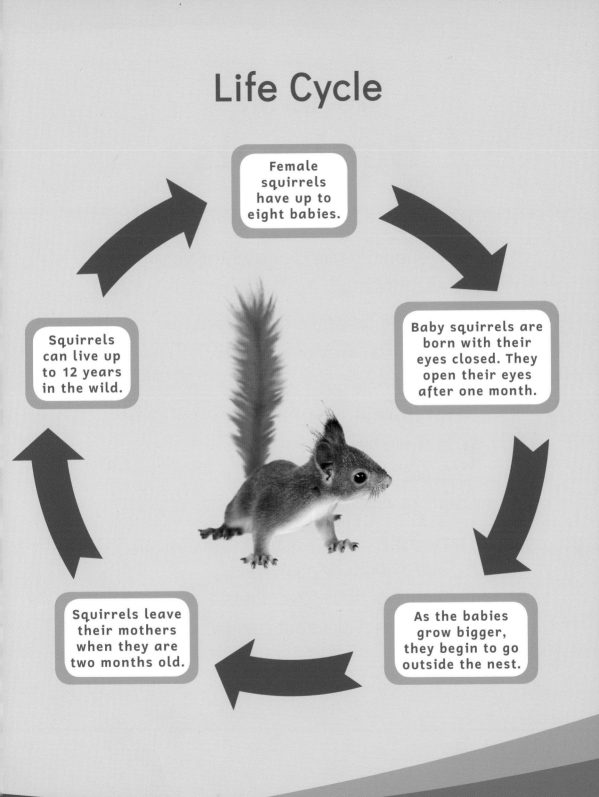

Female squirrels have up to eight babies.

Baby squirrels are born with their eyes closed. They open their eyes after one month.

As the babies grow bigger, they begin to go outside the nest.

Squirrels leave their mothers when they are two months old.

Squirrels can live up to 12 years in the wild.

FOCUS ON
Squirrels

Write your answers on a separate piece of paper.

1. Write a letter to a friend describing how squirrels store food.

2. Is your neighborhood a good place for squirrels to live? Why or why not?

3. How do squirrels use their sharp claws?
   - A. to grow fur
   - B. to climb trees
   - C. to eat acorns

4. What might happen to a forest if there were no more squirrels?
   - A. There would be more trees.
   - B. There would be fewer trees.
   - C. The forest would not change.

Answer key on page 24.

Glossary

buries
Covers something up with dirt.

bushy
Thick and fluffy.

gnaw
To take many small bites.

mammals
Animals that have hair and feed their babies milk.

prepare
To get ready.

twigs
Small sticks.

To Learn More

BOOKS

Lake, G. G. *Gray Squirrels*. North Mankato, MN: Capstone Press, 2017.

O'Brien, Lindsy J. *Squirrels*. Mankato, MN: Creative Education, 2016.

NOTE TO EDUCATORS

Visit **www.focusreaders.com** to find lesson plans, activities, links, and other resources related to this title.

Index

Answer Key: 1. Answers will vary; **2.** Answers will vary; **3.** B; **4.** B